I0446246

"MASTERING LINUX"

A BEGINNER'S GUIDE TO COMMAND LINE AND SYSTEM ADMINISTRATION

NOE TOVAR-MBA

PUBLISHED BY

NOE TOVAR 2023

AMAZON

SCAN FOR AUTHOR PAGE TO ACCESS

OTHER BOOKS BY THIS AUTHOR

For more information, and other titles by this author please scan QR code on previous page.

ISBN: 9798870136295

Imprint: Independently published

Dedication

This book is dedicated to my family, whose unwavering support has been the bedrock of my journey, and to my friends, who have been both critics and confidants, thank you for being the pillars that held me up when the words threatened to crumble.

To the late nights and early mornings, to the moments of inspiration and the struggles of doubt, this dedication is a testament to the rollercoaster of emotions that accompanies the creation of every written word.

May this book serve as a token of gratitude to all those who have touched my life and inspired me to put my thoughts and experience to paper to share what I know and what stirs my curiosity. Your influence is woven into the very fabric of these pages, and I hope that the research, experience and personal thoughts within resonate with the same warmth and wonder that your presence has brought to my world.

With heartfelt appreciation,

With admiration and gratitude,

Noe Tovar-MBA

Table of Contents

WRITER'S NOTE

Dear Readers,

Hey there! Before we dive into the fantastic world of Linux inside these pages, let's have a quick chat. Imagine this book as your cool guide to exploring the world of computers in a super fun and hands-on way. I'm here to make those lines of code and tech jargon a bit less intimidating, more like a friendly conversation.

Listen up, I get it – diving into Linux, an operating system that's like the wizard behind the computer screen, might seem a bit daunting. But guess what? It's not all complicated! Just like learning a new game or mastering a new skill, Linux is an adventure waiting for you.

In this book, I won't throw boring theories at you or make you memorize tons of complicated stuff. Nope, not here! Instead, I'll take you on a journey, step-by-step, unlocking the secrets of Linux in a way that's easy to understand and, more importantly, super exciting.

Think of me as your friendly guide, here to help you learn the ropes of Linux – from the basics of commands to tinkering with the tech wonders hidden inside your computer. And hey, don't worry about making mistakes along the way. That's how we learn best, right?

So, grab your curiosity, bring your enthusiasm, and let's embark on this awesome journey together. By the end of this book, you'll be rocking the

Linux world like a pro and feel empowered to explore even more tech adventures. Let's dive in – the Linux adventure awaits!

MASTERING LINUX:

A Beginner's Guide to Command Line and System Administration

Chapter 1:

INTRODUCTION TO LINUX

Overview of Linux: History and evolution

I'm going to take you on a ride into the universe of Linux – a place where computers become superheroes! So, picture this: a long time ago in the early '90s, when computers were big, slow, and pretty expensive, a super smart guy named Linus Torvalds came up with a brilliant idea.

Imagine Linus as a cool inventor, kind of like a mad scientist but with a friendly vibe. He was just a student like you and me, studying computers in Finland. He wasn't happy with the way things were going in the computer world. Operating systems back then were like secret clubs – closed off and costly.

But Linus wanted something different. Inspired by this cool system called UNIX, he decided to create his own operating system. And guess what? He named it after himself, sort of – combining his name 'Linus' with 'UNIX.' That's how Linux was born!

What made Linux super unique was that it was like a community project, where everyone was invited to join in and help. It's like building an epic treehouse with your pals and sharing it with the entire neighborhood.

The coolest thing about Linux? It's everywhere! From your smartphone to your grandma's fridge (yes, seriously!), this operating system is like the glue that holds so many things together.

As time passed, more and more people joined the Linux gang, adding their own superpowers to make it better. It's like a superhero team-up, but instead of capes, they wore hoodies and carried laptops.

With each new version, Linux got stronger, faster, and more versatile. It's like updating your favorite game – making it cooler with every new level.

Linux isn't owned by one person or company; it's like a giant collaboration party! Think of it as a recipe that everyone can add their secret ingredients to, making it taste even better.

And that, my friend, is the story of Linux – a tech superhero born from the passion of a bunch of super-smart folks, changing the world one line of code at a time.

So, get ready to join the adventure of exploring Linux. We're about to unlock the secrets behind this powerful operating system together!

Linus Torvalds

Understanding open-source software and Linux distributions

So, imagine this: open-source software is like a big recipe book that's open for everyone to read, use, and even add their own special ingredients. Normally, when companies make software, they keep the recipe secret, like a secret formula for a soda. But with open-source, it's like having your favorite cookie recipe and sharing it with all your friends. You can bake it, change it up with extra chocolate chips or nuts, and share your improved recipe with others.

Now, let's talk about Linux distributions. Imagine Linux as a delicious ice cream, and distributions are all the different flavors you can have. Each distribution, like Ubuntu, Fedora, or Debian, is like a different flavor with its own toppings – some are fast and sleek, others come with lots of pre-installed software or have a different look.

Here's a cool chart to visualize it:

Linux Distribution	Description
Ubuntu	Beginner-friendly, widely used, great for everyday tasks
Fedora	Cutting-edge, focused on new features and innovation
Debian	Stable, well-tested, used as a base for many other distros
Arch Linux	Highly customizable, DIY approach, for tech-savvy users
Linux Mint	User-friendly, similar to Windows, with a familiar interface
CentOS	Stable, used in servers and enterprise environments

Think of these distributions like different types of ice cream flavors – some people prefer chocolate, some like vanilla, and others might enjoy something exotic like pistachio or bubblegum!

This chart helps you see at a glance what each distribution offers, making it easier to pick the one that suits your taste or needs best. Just like picking your favorite ice cream flavor, choosing a Linux distribution is all about finding the one that makes you go, "Yep, that's the one for me!"

Now, armed with this chart, you're ready to explore and find the Linux distribution that matches your tech cravings!

For more detail, see the below chart that provides a brief overview of some popular Linux distributions, highlighting their key characteristics and primary use cases:

Linux Distribution	Description	Primary Use Cases
Ubuntu	Beginner-friendly, user-friendly interface	Everyday use, desktop computing, servers
Fedora	Cutting-edge, emphasis on new features and innovation	Development, testing, cutting-edge software
Debian	Stability, reliability, extensive software repositories	Server environments, stability-focused applications
Arch Linux	Highly customizable, do-it-yourself approach	Advanced users, customization, tailored systems
Linux Mint	User-friendly, familiar interface similar to Windows	Desktop use, transition from Windows, multimedia
CentOS	Stable, security-focused, used in enterprise environments	Servers, mission-critical systems, enterprise applications

This chart aims to provide a concise snapshot of each Linux distribution's primary characteristics and intended use cases. It's important to note that each distribution has its strengths, catering to different preferences and requirements. Exploring these distributions further can help users find the one that best aligns with their needs and preferences within the Linux ecosystem.

Advantages and use cases of Linux in the modern computing landscape

welcome to the world of Linux! It's like this fantastic toolbox that holds some of the coolest tools for computing. Let me break down why Linux is such a big deal and how it's changing the way we do things in the world of computers.

First off, Linux is like this superhero of operating systems, and it's free! Yeah, you heard that right – it won't cost you a dime. That means anyone, from students to big companies, can use it without having to worry about paying for licenses. This openness makes it super popular and accessible for everyone.

One of the big reasons folks love Linux is because it's super secure and stable. It's like having a rock-solid fortress protecting your computer from viruses and crashes. That's a big deal, especially when you want your system to work smoothly without any unexpected hiccups.

Now, here's the thing – Linux isn't picky. It runs on almost anything! Your laptop, desktop, servers, smartphones, smart gadgets around your house – you name it. It's like the all-in-one solution that adapts to whatever device you throw at it. This flexibility makes it a go-to choice for tech wizards and companies building new tech stuff.

Let's talk about speed and performance – Linux is lightning fast! It's like the speedster in the computing world, zipping through tasks without breaking a sweat. That's why you'll find Linux powering up servers, supercomputers, and even those tiny computers in your smart devices.

And guess what? Linux isn't just for tech experts. It's for everyone. Whether you're a student learning coding or a business wanting a reliable system for your operations, Linux has something for you. Plus, it's constantly evolving, like a chameleon, adapting to new tech trends and innovations.

Speaking of innovation, Linux is at the heart of it all. Many of the coolest new gadgets and software we see are born on Linux. It's like the playground where developers and tech geniuses gather to create the next big thing.

So, if you want a trustworthy, secure, and versatile system that's free and open for all, Linux is the way to go. It's changing the game in the modern computing landscape, making technology more accessible and powerful for everyone.

That's the magic of Linux – a powerful, open-source superhero that's transforming the world of computing for the better!

Chapter 2:

GETTING STARTED WITH LINUX

Installing Linux: Step-by-step guide for various distributions

So far we have been speaking about the Operating System and distros but I think its time we installed it so you can better understand and practice as the book progresses.

Installation Guide for Ubuntu:

Step 1: Download Ubuntu ISO (https://ubuntu.com/download)

Visit the Ubuntu download page and choose the version (e.g., Ubuntu Desktop) and architecture (32-bit or 64-bit) suitable for your system.

Step 2: Create a Bootable USB Drive

Download a tool like Rufus (for Windows) or BalenaEtcher (for Mac or Linux) to create a bootable USB drive with the Ubuntu ISO file.

Plug in a USB drive (8GB or larger), open the tool, select the downloaded ISO, and create the bootable USB.

Step 3: Boot from USB and Start Installation

Insert the bootable USB into your computer and restart it.

Press the appropriate key (usually F2, F12, or ESC) to access the boot menu and select the USB drive.

Follow the on-screen instructions to start the Ubuntu installation.

Step 4: Installation Process

Choose language, keyboard layout, and select "Install Ubuntu."

Select installation type (Erase disk and install Ubuntu for a clean install or Something else for manual partitioning).

Follow prompts to create a username, password, and other settings.

Let the installation complete, and then restart your computer.

Installation Guide for Fedora:

Step 1: Download Fedora ISO

Go to the Fedora download page and select the version and architecture you need.

Step 2: Create a Bootable USB Drive

Use a tool like BalenaEtcher or Rufus to create a bootable USB drive with the downloaded Fedora ISO file.

Step 3: Boot from USB and Start Installation

Insert the bootable USB into your computer and restart.

Access the boot menu by pressing the corresponding key and select the USB drive.

Choose "Start Fedora Workstation Live" to begin the installation process.

Step 4: Installation Process

Launch the installer from the live environment.

Follow the prompts to choose language, keyboard layout, and installation destination.

Set up user accounts, passwords, and other configurations as needed.

Proceed with the installation and restart your system after completion.

Installation Guide for Debian:

Step 1: Download Debian ISO

Visit the Debian download page and select the appropriate version and architecture.

Step 2: Create a Bootable USB Drive

Use a tool like Rufus or BalenaEtcher to create a bootable USB drive with the Debian ISO file.

Step 3: Boot from USB and Start Installation

Insert the bootable USB and restart your computer.

Access the boot menu and select the USB drive to boot into the Debian installer.

Step 4: Installation Process

Choose language, location, keyboard layout, and proceed with the installation.

Select the installation type, partition your disk, and set up user accounts.

Let the installation process complete and restart your computer.

Visual Installation Steps Chart:

Distribution	Download ISO	Create Bootable USB	Boot from USB	Installation Process
Ubuntu	Download	Tool: Rufus/BalenaEtcher	Access boot menu	Follow on-screen prompts
Fedora	Download	Tool: Rufus/BalenaEtcher	Access boot menu	Follow live environment installer
Debian	Download	Tool: Rufus/BalenaEtcher	Access boot menu	Follow Debian installer prompts

This chart summarizes the key steps for installing Ubuntu, Fedora, and Debian, making it easier to understand and follow along visually.

Remember, installation steps might slightly vary based on system configurations, so it's always good to refer to the official installation guides provided by each distribution for detailed and updated instructions.

Good luck with your Linux installation adventure!

Scan QR code to see video demos on installing and more.

Introduction to the Linux terminal and basic commands

Welcome to the world of Linux commands – the magical land of the terminal! Think of the terminal as a superpower that lets you communicate directly with your computer using text commands. It might look a bit intimidating at first, but trust me, it's like learning spells in a magical language!

Terminal Basics:

Opening the Terminal: To enter the terminal, simply search for "Terminal" in your applications or press Ctrl + Alt + T (on most distributions) to summon it.

Command Structure: Commands in the terminal usually follow this structure:

```css
command [options] [arguments]
```

Now, let's dive into some basic commands and what they do:

Basic Terminal Commands:

1. ls - List Directory Contents:

This command shows you the files and folders in your current directory.

2. cd - Change Directory:

Use cd followed by a directory name to move around.

```bash
cd Documents
```

3. mkdir - Make Directory:

Creates a new directory.

```arduino
mkdir NewFolder
```

4. touch - Create a New File:

Makes a new empty file.

```bash
touch new_file.txt
```

5. rm - Remove/Delete:

Deletes a file or directory. Be cautious with this command!

```bash
rm file.txt
```

6. pwd - Print Working Directory:

Shows the path of the current directory you're in.

```bash
pwd
```

Visual Command Explanation Chart:

Command	Function	Example
`ls`	List directory contents	`ls`
`cd`	Change directory	`cd Documents`
`mkdir`	Make directory	`mkdir NewFolder`
`touch`	Create a new file	`touch new_file.txt`
`rm`	Remove/delete file or directory	`rm file.txt`
`pwd`	Print current directory path	`pwd`

This visual chart illustrates some fundamental commands in the Linux terminal. Each command has its unique function, making it easier to understand and remember while navigating through the terminal.

Practice these commands in your terminal playground, and before you know it, you'll be casting spells in this command-line wizardry like a pro!

This introduction and visual command explanation aim to provide a friendly and clear understanding of basic Linux terminal commands. Feel free to explore more commands and unleash the power of the terminal at your own pace!

Navigating the file system: File paths, directories, and permissions

Navigating the file system in Linux is like exploring a digital world filled with folders, files, and permissions. Let me guide you through this adventure visually to make it easy to understand.

Navigating the File System:

Hey, fellow explorer! Imagine the file system in Linux as a giant map, and I'm here to help you read it like a seasoned cartographer.

1. File Paths:

Absolute Paths: These show the full route from the root directory (/) to a file or folder. For example: /home/user/Documents.

Relative Paths: These describe the location of a file or folder relative to the current directory. For instance, if you're in /home/user, the relative path to Documents could be Documents or ../user/Documents.

2. Directories:

Root Directory (/): It's like the top-level parent directory. Everything branches out from here.

Home Directory (~ or /home/user): This is your personal space in the system. It's where your files and folders are by default.

3. Permissions:

File Permissions: Each file and folder has permissions indicating who can read, write, or execute them. They are represented as three groups: owner, group, and others, with permission types: read (r), write (w), and execute (x).

Visual File System Explanation Chart:

Concept	Description	Example
Absolute Path	Full path starting from the root directory `/`	`/home/user/Documents`
Relative Path	Path relative to the current directory	`Documents` or `../user/Documents`
Root Directory	Top-level parent directory	`/`
Home Directory	Personal space for users	`~` or `/home/user`
File Permissions	Permissions for reading (`r`), writing (`w`), and executing (`x`) files and directories	`rwxr-xr--`

This chart visually explains file paths, directories, and permissions in the Linux file system. Understanding these concepts will help you navigate through the digital landscape with ease.

Remember, each directory and file has its place in this file system map, and knowing how to navigate and understand permissions will empower you to explore and manage your files confidently!

This Following visual explanation aims to provide a clear understanding of navigating the Linux file system. Feel free to refer to this chart as you explore and maneuver through directories and files in your Linux adventure!

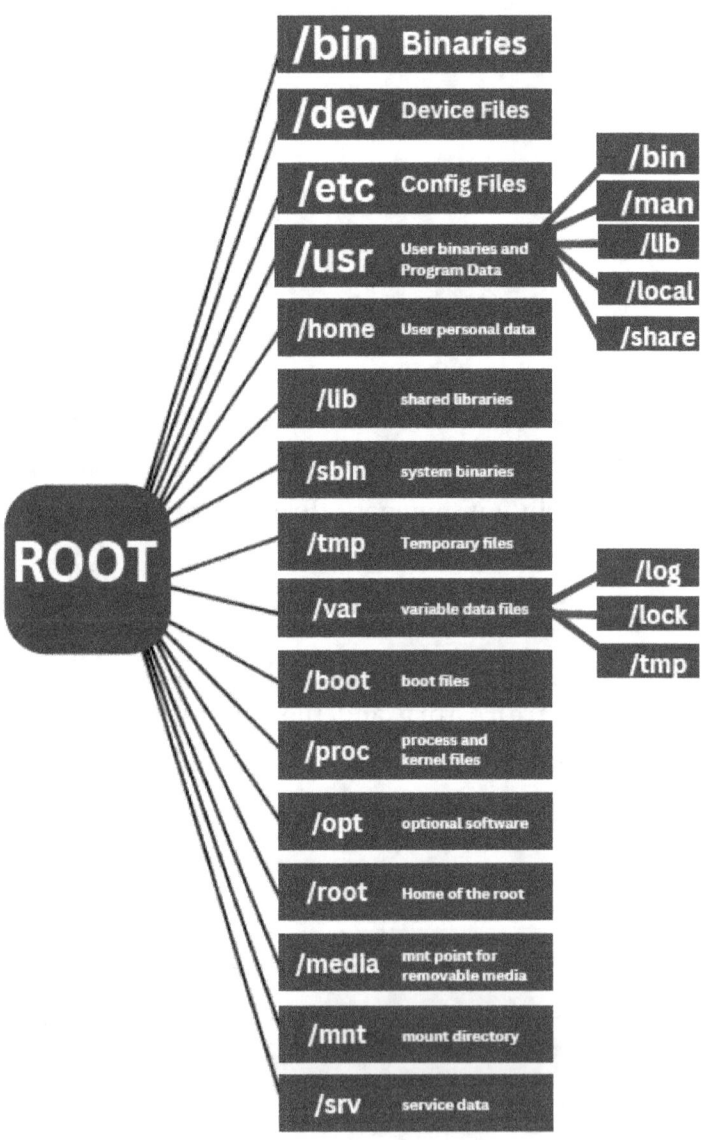

LINUX FILE STUCTURE

This Following visual explanation aims to provide a clear understanding of navigating the Linux file system in support of the previous illustration.

/bin	Binaries: Repository for fundamental binaries, playing a vital role in both the boot and repair operations of Linux systems.
/dev	Device Files: Connection point for device files, facilitating communication between the Linux system and hardware.
/etc	Configuration Files: Central hub for system configuration files, governing the behavior of various applications in Linux.
/usr	User Binaries: Repository housing user-related binaries, libraries, documentation, and source code for Linux systems.
/home	User Home Directories: Collection of user home directories, housing individual user data in the Linux file system.
/lib	Libraries: Crucial repository for shared libraries, foundational for both system and application functionality in Linux
/sbin	System Binaries: Essential repository for critical system binaries crucial for Linux system recovery and maintenance.
/tmp	Temporary Files: Temporary holding ground for transient files and directories in the Linux file system.
/var	Variable Data: Dynamic storage for data, logs, and variable content crucial for Linux system functionality.
/boot	Boot Loader Files: Storage space containing essential boot loader files, critical for initiating the startup process in Linux systems.
/proc	Process Information: Virtual directory providing comprehensive information about running processes in Linux systems.
/opt	Optimal Software: Organized repository for optional software packages, promoting streamlined integration in the Linux system.
/root	Root Home: Home directory for the superuser, housing vital configuration files for Linux system management.
/media	Removable Media: Storage space for mount points dedicated to removable media devices within the Linux file system.
/mnt	Mount Points: Directory serving as mount points for external devices, facilitating seamless integration into Linux systems.
/srv	Service Data: Dedicated space for service-specific data, ensuring optimal functionality for various Linux applications.

CHAPTER 3:
COMMAND LINE ESSENTIALS

Working with files and directories: ls, cd, mkdir, rm, cp, mv, etc.

Let's go through some essential commands in a relaxed and easy-to-understand way:

Working with Files and Directories in Linux:

Hey there! Imagine your computer's files and folders like your room's stuff. You've got clothes, books, and gadgets, right? Linux helps you organize and manage them with cool commands.

1. ls - List Directory Contents:

This command is like peeking into your closet to see what's inside. When I type ls, it shows me all the files and folders in my current directory.

2. cd - Change Directory:

If I want to move around in my house, I use cd! Let's say I want to go from the bedroom to the kitchen. I type cd kitchen to move there. Easy, right?

3. mkdir - Make Directory:

Making a new folder is like creating a new storage space for my stuff. To create a folder named "projects," I use mkdir projects. Now I have a place for all my project stuff!

4. rm - Remove/Delete:

Sometimes I need to get rid of things I don't need anymore. rm helps me delete files. But be careful! It's like throwing out old clothes. For example, rm old_file.txt will delete that file.

5. cp - Copy:

Just like making copies of notes, cp lets me copy files. If I have a file named "important.txt" and want to copy it, I'd type cp important.txt backup/important_backup.txt.

6. mv - Move/Rename:

Moving files is like rearranging my room. With mv, I can move files to different folders. If I want to rename "file1.txt" to "newfile.txt," I'd type mv file1.txt newfile.txt.

7. pwd - Print Working Directory:

It's like knowing your location on Google Maps! When I type pwd, Linux shows me the full path of where I am in my computer.

Remember:

Use ls to see what's there.

cd helps you move around.

mkdir creates new spaces.

rm deletes stuff, so be careful!

cp copies files.

mv moves or renames files.

pwd tells you where you are.

Text file manipulation using commands like cat, grep, awk, sed

Text file manipulation in Linux using commands like cat, grep, awk, and sed is like having magic powers to handle and transform text effortlessly. Let's explore these commands in a relatable way:

Text File Manipulation with Linux Commands:

Hey, picture your text files as stories or essays. These Linux commands help me read, search, and edit those files just like a word wizard!

1. cat - Concatenate Files and Display:

cat is my go-to command when I want to see the content of a file. It's like opening a book to read. I use it like this: cat file.txt. It shows everything in the file right in the terminal.

2. grep - Search Text Patterns:

When I need to find something specific in a file, grep is my detective. If I want to find the word "apple" in a file named "fruits.txt," I'd type grep 'apple' fruits.txt. It shows me the lines containing "apple."

3. awk - Text Processing:

awk is my magic wand for text processing. I can use it to extract specific information. For example, I can print the first column of a file using awk '{print $1}' file.txt. It's like creating customized reports!

4. sed - Stream Editor:

With sed, I can do text transformations. Let's say I want to replace all "hello" with "hi" in a file. I'd do sed 's/hello/hi/g' file.txt. It's like having a find-and-replace superpower.

Visual Representation in Tables:

Let's summarize these commands for clarity:

Command	Function	Example Usage
`cat`	Display file content	`cat file.txt`
`grep`	Search text patterns	`grep 'apple' fruits.txt`
`awk`	Text processing, extracting information	`awk '{print $1}' file.txt`
`sed`	Stream editor, text transformations	`sed 's/hello/hi/g' file.txt`

These commands make text file handling in Linux super convenient! They help me read, search, extract, and transform text effortlessly. Practicing them turns me into a text magician in the Linux world!

Understanding pipes, redirection, and filters to process command output

Picture your command output as a flow of information. Pipes, redirection, and filters help me manage this flow, shaping it the way I want.

1. Pipes (|) - Connecting Commands:

Pipes are like pipelines that connect commands together, passing the output of one command as input to another. It's as simple as using | between commands. For instance, command1 | command2 directs the output of command1 to command2.

2. Redirection (>, >>, <) - Managing Input/Output:

Redirection is like directing the flow of information to or from a file or command.

> redirects output to a file. For example, command > output.txt saves the output of command to output.txt.

>> appends output to a file. It's like adding information to an existing file. For instance, command >> output.txt.

< redirects input from a file. Using command < input.txt sends input.txt as input to command.

3. Filters (grep, sed, awk, sort, uniq, etc.) - Filtering Output:

Filters help me refine and process command output.

grep searches for specific patterns in text.

sed performs text transformations.

awk processes text based on rules.

sort arranges lines alphabetically or numerically.

uniq filters out adjacent matching lines.

Visual Representation in Chart:

Here's a chart summarizing these concepts:

Concept	Symbol	Functionality	Example
Pipes	`` ` ``	`` ` ``	Connects commands, passes output as input
Redirection	`` `>` ``, `` `>>` ``, `` `<` ``	Manages input/output to/from files	`` `command > output.txt` ``
Filters	`` `grep` ``, `` `sed` ``, `` `awk` ``, `` `sort` ``, `` `uniq` ``, etc.	Refines and processes command output	`` `grep 'keyword' file.txt` ``

These tools allow me to be creative and precise with the output of Linux commands. By combining them, I can shape, filter, and direct information flow exactly as I need!

With pipes, redirection, and filters, I can create command workflows that efficiently manipulate and manage data in the Linux terminal. They're like magic wands that make working with command output flexible and powerful!

Scan QR code to see video demos on the cat command!

and the redirect command and more.

CHAPTER 4:
SYSTEM BASICS

System architecture: Understanding processes, threads, and multitasking

Picture your computer's work as a team effort. Processes, threads, and multitasking are like different aspects of teamwork happening inside your system.

1. Processes:

Think of a process as a task your computer runs. Each process has its own space and resources. They can be a program, like a music player or a web browser. I can start or stop processes using commands like ps or kill.

2. Threads:

Threads are like small tasks within a process. They share resources and memory with other threads in the same process. They help in parallel execution within a process. It's like several workers in a team handling different parts of a project.

3. Multitasking:

Multitasking is doing multiple things at once. Your computer achieves this by switching between processes or threads very quickly. It's like juggling different tasks, making it seem like they're happening simultaneously.

Concept	Description	Example
Processes	Tasks running independently	Music player, web browser
Threads	Smaller tasks within a process	Handling UI, I/O tasks
Multitasking	Simultaneous execution of multiple processes/threads	Listening to music, browsing

This chart helps visualize how processes, threads, and multitasking work together in the system. Processes run independently, threads handle tasks within processes, and multitasking juggles multiple activities simultaneously.

By understanding how processes and threads collaborate while multitasking, we get a clearer picture of how our computer efficiently manages tasks. It's like a well-organized team, each doing their part to keep things running smoothly in the Linux world!

Managing users and groups: useradd, usermod, passwd, etc.

Managing users and groups in Linux is like organizing different teams and granting them access to resources. Let's explore commands like useradd, usermod, passwd, and more in an easy-to-understand way, and then I'll provide a hands-on exercise to solidify the learning.

Managing Users and Groups in Linux:

Hey! Think of users as members of a club, and groups as different clubs within the system. These commands help me manage who's in which club and what they can do.

1. useradd - Add Users:

useradd is like creating a new club member. It adds a new user to the system. For example, useradd john creates a user named "john."

2. usermod - Modify User:

usermod helps me modify user details like their home directory or group. If I want to change John's primary group to "developers," I'd do usermod -g developers john.

3. passwd - Set Password:

passwd is like giving a secret code to access the club. When I run passwd john, it prompts me to set a password for the user "john."

4. groupadd - Create Groups:

groupadd is like creating a new club in the system. For instance, groupadd developers creates a group named "developers."

5. userdel - Delete Users:

When a club member leaves, I use userdel to remove them. For example, userdel john deletes the user "john."

Visual Representation in Chart:

Let's summarize these commands for better understanding:

Command	Functionality	Example Usage
`useradd`	Add new users to the system	`useradd john`
`usermod`	Modify user details	`usermod -g developers john`
`passwd`	Set password for a user	`passwd john`
`groupadd`	Create new groups	`groupadd developers`
`userdel`	Remove users from the system	`userdel john`

This chart visually summarizes the functions of each command for managing users and groups in Linux.

Hands-On Exercise:

Now, here's an exercise to practice:

Create a new user named "testuser" using useradd.

Set a password for "testuser" using passwd.

Create a new group named "testgroup" using groupadd.

Add "testuser" to the "testgroup" using usermod.

Finally, delete the "testuser" using userdel.

This hands-on exercise will help solidify your understanding of managing users and groups in Linux.

Learning by doing is the best way to understand these commands! Practice this exercise, and you'll feel more confident managing users and groups in your Linux system!

Exploring system information and monitoring tools: top, ps, df, du, etc.

Exploring system information and monitoring tools in Linux is like having a dashboard to check the heartbeat of your system. Let's explore commands like top, ps, df, du, and more in an easy-to-understand way, and then I'll provide a hands-on exercise to reinforce the learning.

Exploring System Information and Monitoring Tools in Linux:

Hey there! Think of these commands as tools to peek inside your system's health and track what's happening under the hood.

1. top - Display System Activity:

top is like a live feed showing what's running on your system. It displays CPU usage, memory usage, and running processes in real-time.

2. ps - Display Process Status:

When I use ps, it's like getting a snapshot of running processes. For instance, ps aux shows all processes on the system.

3. df - Display Filesystem Usage:

df helps me check how much space is used on different filesystems. It's like checking how much space is left in your drawers or closets.

4. du - Display Disk Usage:

du is like examining how much space each directory uses. For example, du -sh /home/user shows the size of the user's home directory.

Visual Representation in Chart:

Let's create a chart to visualize these commands:

Command	Functionality	Example Usage
`top`	Real-time system activity	`top`
`ps`	Display process status	`ps aux`
`df`	Display filesystem usage	`df -h`
`du`	Display disk usage	`du -sh /home/user`

This chart summarizes the functions of each command for exploring system information and monitoring in Linux.

Hands-On Exercise:

Now, here's an exercise to practice:

Use top to monitor system activity in real-time.

Use ps aux to list all processes running on the system.

Use df -h to display the disk space usage on all filesystems.

Use du -sh /path/to/directory to check the disk space used by a specific directory.

This hands-on exercise will give you a practical understanding of these commands and how they provide system information and monitoring in Linux.

These commands act as your system's detective, allowing you to monitor performance and track what's happening in your Linux environment. Practice this exercise to get a feel for these tools and gain confidence in system monitoring!

Be sure to scan the QR code at the end for a bonus eBook with additional commands like the ones in this illustration.

DISK USAGE

```
# Show free and used space on mounted
filesystems
df -h

# Show free and used inodes on mounted
filesystems
df -i

# Display disks partitions sizes and types
fdisk -l

# Display disk usage for all files and
directories in human readable format
du -ah

# Display total disk usage off the current
directory
du -sh
```

CHAPTER 5:
FILESYSTEM AND STORAGE MANAGEMENT.

Filesystem hierarchy standard (FHS) and its significance

Think of FHS as a detailed blueprint that organizes where different types of files should live within the Linux system. This standard ensures consistency and helps programs find what they need.

Significance of FHS:

FHS creates a uniform directory structure, ensuring:

Consistency: All Linux distributions follow this structure, making it easier for users and developers to navigate.

Clarity: It defines specific directories for certain types of files, like /bin for essential binaries, /etc for configuration files, /var for variable data, and so on.

Ease of Development: Developers can rely on standardized paths, making software development and compatibility across distributions smoother.

Visual Representation in Chart:

Let's create a chart to visualize the main directories defined by FHS:

Disk management: Formatting, partitioning, mounting drives

Directory	Description	Example Content
`/`	Root directory	`/bin`, `/etc`, `/var`, `/home`, etc.
`/bin`	Essential system binaries	`ls`, `cp`, `mv`, `cat`, etc.
`/etc`	System configuration files	`passwd`, `hostname`, `network`, etc.
`/var`	Variable data	Log files, databases, emails, etc.
`/home`	User home directories	`/home/user1`, `/home/user2`, etc.
`/tmp`	Temporary files	Temporary cache, temporary downloads

This chart illustrates some key directories specified by FHS and their purposes within the Linux filesystem hierarchy.

Hands-On Exercise:

Now, here's an exercise to practice:

Explore the contents of the /etc directory using ls /etc.

Navigate to your home directory using cd ~ and create a new directory named "my_projects" using mkdir my_projects.

Check the disk space usage of the /var directory using du -sh /var.

List the contents of the /bin directory using ls /bin.

This hands-on exercise will familiarize you with navigating through FHS directories and understanding their contents.

Understanding FHS is like having a map to efficiently locate and organize files within a Linux system. Practice this exercise to get a practical grasp of these important directory structures!

Introduction to Filesystem Types: ext4, NTFS, FAT, etc.

Think of filesystem types as different languages your computer uses to organize and manage data on storage devices. Each has its own features and capabilities.

1. ext4 (Fourth Extended Filesystem):

Linux Native: ext4 is the default filesystem for most Linux distributions.

Features: It supports large file sizes, journaling for improved reliability, and efficient handling of large filesystems.

Usage: Suitable for Linux systems due to its performance and reliability.

2. NTFS (New Technology File System):

Windows Native: NTFS is the default filesystem for Windows operating systems.

Features: It supports large files, file compression, file permissions, and journaling.

Compatibility: It's well-suited for Windows but can be read by Linux and macOS with third-party tools.

3. FAT (File Allocation Table):

Older Format: FAT comes in various versions like FAT12, FAT16, FAT32.

Features: It's simple, compatible with various systems, but has limitations on file size and partition size.

Usage: Commonly used for USB drives, memory cards, and in legacy systems.

4. exFAT (Extended File Allocation Table):

Extended FAT: exFAT is an enhanced version of FAT, addressing its limitations.

Features: Supports large files, large volumes, and is compatible with different operating systems.

Usage: Suitable for flash drives, external hard drives, and other storage devices.

Visual Representation in Chart:

Let's create a chart to visualize these filesystem types:

Filesystem Type	Description	Features	Usage
ext4	Linux native filesystem	Large file support, journaling, reliability	Linux systems
NTFS	Windows native filesystem	Large files, permissions, journaling	Windows systems
FAT	Older filesystem format	Simplicity, compatibility, limitations	USB drives, legacy systems
exFAT	Extended FAT format	Large files, large volumes, cross-platform	Flash drives, external HDDs

↓

This chart summarizes the main features and typical usage of different filesystem types for easy understanding.

Hands-On Exercise:

Now, here's an exercise to practice:

Format a USB drive with the FAT32 filesystem.

Create a text file on the USB drive.

Copy the text file to your Linux system and then to a Windows system.

Compare how each system handles the file on the USB drive formatted with FAT32.

This exercise will help you understand how different filesystems are used across various operating systems and their compatibility.

Different filesystems offer different features and are suited for specific purposes. Experimenting with formatting and file handling across various systems will provide a hands-on understanding of their functionalities and compatibility!

CHAPTER 6:
PACKAGE MANAGEMENT

Understanding package managers: apt, yum, dnf, etc.

Understanding package managers like apt, yum, dnf, and others is like having a shopping assistant who helps you find, install, and manage software on your Linux system. Let's delve into these package managers, their characteristics, and differences in an engaging way.

Understanding Package Managers:

Hey there! Think of package managers as your software helpers, making it easy to install, update, and remove programs on your Linux system. Each has its own way of managing packages.

1. apt (Advanced Package Tool):

Debian-Based Systems: apt is the go-to package manager for Debian-based distributions like Ubuntu.

Features: It's known for dependency resolution, simple usage, and a vast repository of software.

Commands: Common commands include apt-get, apt-cache, and aptitude.

2. yum (Yellowdog Updater Modified):

Red Hat-Based Systems: yum was the package manager for older Red Hat-based systems like CentOS 6 and earlier versions.

Features: It handled package dependencies, updates, and installations.

Legacy: In newer Red Hat-based systems like CentOS 7 and 8, yum has been replaced by dnf.

3. dnf (Dandified YUM):

Modern Red Hat-Based Systems: dnf is the successor of yum in newer Red Hat-based distributions like CentOS 8 and Fedora.

Features: It offers better performance, improved dependency resolution, and a cleaner command structure compared to yum.

Commands: Similar to yum but with enhanced functionality.

4. Others:

Other package managers like pacman for Arch Linux, zypper for openSUSE, and apk for Alpine Linux have their own unique features and commands suited for their respective distributions.

Visual Representation in Chart:

Let's create a chart to visualize these package managers:

Package Manager	Distribution	Features	Common Commands
`apt`	Debian-based	Dependency resolution, vast repositories	`apt-get`, `apt-cache`
`yum`	Older Red Hat	Dependency handling, updates	Deprecated in newer versions
`dnf`	Modern Red Hat	Enhanced performance, clean commands	`dnf install`, `dnf update`
Others	Distribution-specific	Unique features and commands	Varies by distribution

This chart summarizes the main package managers, their distributions, features, and commonly used commands for managing software on Linux.

Hands-On Exercise:

Now, here's an exercise to practice:

On a Debian-based system (like Ubuntu), use apt to install a package of your choice.

On a Red Hat-based system (like CentOS 8), use dnf to update all installed packages.

Compare the commands and output of apt and dnf to see how they differ in usage and presentation.

This exercise will help you get hands-on experience with different package managers and understand their usage on different Linux distributions.

Exploring different package managers is like navigating different stores in a mall—they have their own styles, but ultimately, they help you find and manage software for your system. Experimenting with different commands on various distributions will solidify your understanding of package management in Linux!

Installing, updating, and removing software packages

Think of managing software packages in Linux as adding, updating, and removing apps from your device—just a bit more command line magic!

1. Installing Packages:

Adding New Apps: To install software, I use the command specific to my package manager. For example:

With apt: sudo apt-get install packageName

With dnf: sudo dnf install packageName

2. Updating Packages:

Keeping Apps Current: To update installed software to the latest version:

With apt: sudo apt-get update and then sudo apt-get upgrade

With dnf: sudo dnf update

3. Removing Packages:

Spring Cleaning: When I want to remove software I no longer need:

With apt: sudo apt-get remove packageName

With dnf: sudo dnf remove packageName

Visual Representation in Chart:

Let's create a chart to visualize these actions:

Action	Command	Example Usage
Install	`apt-get install packageName`	`sudo apt-get install firefox`
Update	`apt-get update` and `apt-get upgrade`	`sudo apt-get update` followed by `sudo apt-get upgrade`
Remove	`apt-get remove packageName`	`sudo apt-get remove firefox`

This chart summarizes the commands for installing, updating, and removing software packages using apt-get as an example for clarity.

Hands-On Exercise:

Now, here's an exercise to practice:

Using apt-get on a Debian-based system:

Install a new package (e.g., sudo apt-get install neofetch).

Update all installed packages (e.g., sudo apt-get update and sudo apt-get upgrade).

Remove the newly installed package (e.g., sudo apt-get remove neofetch).

Using dnf on a Red Hat-based system:

Install a new package (e.g., sudo dnf install htop).

Update all installed packages (e.g., sudo dnf update).

Remove the newly installed package (e.g., sudo dnf remove htop).

This exercise will give you hands-on experience with installing, updating, and removing software packages using different package managers on Linux.

Managing software packages on Linux is like maintaining your app library—you can easily add, update, and remove software to keep your system fresh and efficient. Practice these commands, and you'll become a pro at managing software packages on your Linux system!

Repository management and package dependencies

Think of repositories as libraries that store software packages, and package dependencies as the interconnected parts needed for those packages to work together seamlessly.

1. Repository Management:

Repositories: They are online libraries that store software packages. Each distribution has its set of official repositories.

Adding Repositories: To add a new repository, I use commands specific to my package manager:

With apt: sudo add-apt-repository repositoryName

With dnf: sudo dnf config-manager --add-repo repositoryURL

2. Package Dependencies:

Dependencies: They are additional software or libraries required for a package to work correctly.

Resolution: Package managers automatically handle dependencies when installing or updating software, ensuring all necessary parts are present.

Visual Representation in Chart:

Let's create a chart to visualize repository management and package dependencies:

Action	Command	Example Usage
Add Repository	`add-apt-repository repositoryName`	`sudo add-apt-repository ppa:example/exampleRepository`
	`dnf config-manager -- add-repo repositoryURL`	`sudo dnf config-manager --add-repo https://example.com/repo.repo`
Handle Dependencies	Automatically managed by package manager	`sudo apt-get install packageName`

his chart summarizes the commands for adding repositories and how package managers handle dependencies during package installation using apt and dnf as examples.

Hands-On Exercise:

Now, here's an exercise to practice:

On a Debian-based system:

Add a new repository using add-apt-repository.

Install a package from the added repository using apt-get.

Observe how dependencies are managed during the installation process.

On a Red Hat-based system:

Add a repository using dnf config-manager.

Install a package from the added repository using dnf.

Check the installed package's dependencies using rpm -qR packageName.

This exercise will provide hands-on experience with adding repositories, installing packages, and understanding how package managers handle dependencies on different Linux distributions.

Managing repositories and package dependencies is like ensuring you have access to the right books and all the necessary chapters to build a complete story. By practicing these commands, you'll become adept at managing software sources and ensuring smooth package installations on your Linux system!

CHAPTER 7:
NETWORKING BASICS

Understanding network basics in Linux is like learning the foundation of how information travels and communicates in a digital world. Let's kickstart this chapter with an introduction that simplifies these concepts, and then I'll provide a hands-on exercise to reinforce your learning.

Introduction to Network Basics:

Hey there! Imagine networks as the intricate web that connects devices, allowing them to share information and communicate across the digital realm. In this chapter, we'll unravel the fundamental elements of networking in Linux, exploring how devices find each other, exchange data, and collaborate seamlessly. From understanding IP addresses to deciphering the role of DNS and DHCP, we'll navigate through these essential concepts, giving you the keys to unlock the mysteries of networking in your Linux environment.

Visual Representation in Chart:

Let's create a chart to visualize the key components of network basics:

Concept	Description	Example
IP Addressing	Unique addresses for devices on a network	IPv4: 192.168.1.1, IPv6: 2001:0db8:85a3:0000:0000:8a2e:0370:7334
DNS	Translates domain names to IP addresses	google.com -> 172.217.12.14
DHCP	Automates IP address assignment	Assigning IPs to devices

This chart summarizes the essential concepts we'll explore in this chapter, providing a visual guide to understanding network basics in Linux.

Hands-On Exercise:

Now, here's an exercise to dive deeper into network basics:

Set up a basic network configuration:

Use commands like ifconfig or ip addr to view current network settings.

Modify the network configuration files to assign a static IP address to your Linux system.

Restart the network service and verify the changes.

Perform DNS resolution:

Use the nslookup or dig command to query DNS servers for the IP address of a domain (e.g., nslookup openai.com).

By completing this exercise, you'll gain practical experience in configuring network settings and utilizing DNS resolution, solidifying your understanding of network basics in Linux.

Embark on this journey to demystify the core elements of networking in Linux. By practicing these exercises, you'll not only comprehend the basics but also gain hands-on expertise in configuring and understanding networks within your Linux environment!

Networking concepts in Linux: IP addressing, DNS, DHCP

Think of networking in Linux as managing addresses, looking up names, and automating connections to navigate the digital world effectively.

1. IP Addressing:

Addresses for Communication: IP (Internet Protocol) addresses are like unique house addresses for devices on a network.

IPv4 and IPv6: IPv4 uses a 32-bit address format (e.g., 192.168.1.1), while IPv6 uses a 128-bit address format (e.g., 2001:0db8:85a3:0000:0000:8a2e:0370:7334).

Subnetting: Dividing large networks into smaller ones for better organization and management.

2. DNS (Domain Name System):

Address Translation: DNS is like a digital phonebook, translating human-readable domain names (like google.com) into IP addresses.

Domain Hierarchy: It follows a hierarchical structure with domain levels like top-level domains (TLDs), domain names, and subdomains.

3. DHCP (Dynamic Host Configuration Protocol):

Automated Network Configuration: DHCP is like an automated system assigning IP addresses to devices when they connect to a network.

Lease Management: It leases IP addresses for a specific duration, ensuring efficient use of available addresses.

Visual Representation in Chart:

Let's create a chart to visualize these networking concepts:

Concept	Description	Example
IP Addressing	Unique addresses for devices on a network	IPv4: 192.168.1.1, IPv6: 2001:0db8:85a3:0000:0000:8a2e:0370:7334
DNS	Translates domain names to IP addresses	google.com -> 172.217.12.14
DHCP	Automates IP address assignment	Assigning IPs to devices

This chart summarizes the key networking concepts in Linux, their roles, and examples for better understanding.

Hands-On Exercise:

Now, here's an exercise to practice:

Configure a static IP address on your Linux system:

Use commands like ifconfig or ip addr to check your current network configuration.

Edit the network configuration files (e.g., /etc/network/interfaces or /etc/sysconfig/network-scripts/ifcfg-*) to set a static IP address.

Apply the changes and restart the network service (service networking restart or systemctl restart network).

Use DNS resolution to translate a domain name to an IP address:

Use the nslookup or dig command to query DNS servers for the IP address of a domain (e.g., nslookup google.com).

This exercise will help you understand and practice IP addressing, configuring networks, and utilizing DNS resolution on your Linux system.

Understanding networking concepts in Linux is like having a map to navigate and communicate across the digital landscape. By practicing these commands and configurations, you'll gain a deeper understanding of how networking functions in your Linux environment!

Configuring network interfaces using ifconfig, ip, and nmcli

Think of network interfaces as the gates that control the flow of information in and out of your Linux system. I use different commands to manage these interfaces efficiently.

1. ifconfig Command:

Legacy Tool: ifconfig was traditionally used to configure network interfaces but is now considered outdated in some Linux distributions.

Usage: I can view, configure, or bring up/down network interfaces using commands like ifconfig eth0 up or ifconfig eth0 192.168.1.2 netmask 255.255.255.0.

2. ip Command:

Modern Replacement: ip is the go-to command for configuring network interfaces in modern Linux distributions.

Versatility: With ip, I can perform a wide range of tasks like viewing interface details (ip addr show), assigning IP addresses (ip addr add), or bringing interfaces up/down (ip link set).

3. nmcli Command:

NetworkManager Tool: nmcli is part of NetworkManager, providing a command-line interface for managing network connections.

Usage: It allows me to view connection details (nmcli connection show), bring up/down connections (nmcli connection up), or modify connection settings (nmcli connection modify).

Visual Representation in Chart:

Let's create a chart to visualize these commands for configuring network interfaces:

Command	Description	Example Usage
`ifconfig`	Legacy tool for interface configuration	`ifconfig eth0 up`, `ifconfig eth0 192.168.1.2 netmask 255.255.255.0`
`ip`	Modern and versatile interface tool	`ip addr show`, `ip addr add`, `ip link set`
`nmcli`	NetworkManager command-line interface	`nmcli connection show`, `nmcli connection up`, `nmcli connection modify`

This chart summarizes the commands for configuring network interfaces in Linux using ifconfig, ip, and nmcli, providing a visual guide for easy understanding.

Hands-On Exercise:

Now, here's an exercise to practice configuring network interfaces:

Using ip command:

Use ip addr show to display current network interface details.

Assign a static IP address to an interface using ip addr add.

Bring up and down an interface using ip link set.

Utilizing nmcli command:

View available connections with nmcli connection show.

Modify connection settings (e.g., change IP address or DNS) using nmcli connection modify.

Bring up and down a connection using nmcli connection up and nmcli connection down.

By completing this exercise, you'll gain practical experience in configuring network interfaces using different commands on your Linux system.

Configuring network interfaces is like setting up pathways for seamless information flow within your Linux environment. Through these exercises, you'll become adept at managing network interfaces using various commands, ensuring smooth communication within your system!

Troubleshooting network connectivity issues

troubleshooting network connectivity issues is like being a detective, uncovering and resolving issues that hinder smooth communication between devices. Let's delve into troubleshooting network connectivity problems in Linux, visualize common issues and their resolutions, and then I'll provide a hands-on exercise to reinforce your troubleshooting skills.

Troubleshooting Network Connectivity Issues:

Hey there! Imagine your network as a complex web of connections where sometimes issues arise, causing disruptions in communication. I often use diagnostic commands and methods to identify and fix these problems efficiently.

1. Checking Interface Status:

Using ip or ifconfig: I verify if the network interface is up (ip link show or ifconfig) to ensure it's active and properly configured.

2. Investigating IP Configuration:

Using ip or ifconfig: I check the assigned IP address, subnet mask, and gateway settings to ensure they are correct (ip addr show or ifconfig).

3. Testing Connectivity:

Using ping: I employ the ping command to test connectivity to a specific IP address or domain name (ping 8.8.8.8 or ping google.com) to check for connectivity issues.

4. Diagnosing DNS Problems:

Using nslookup or dig: I check DNS resolution by querying DNS servers for domain name resolution (nslookup openai.com or dig openai.com) to identify DNS-related issues.

Visual Representation in Chart:

Let's create a chart to visualize common troubleshooting steps for network connectivity issues:

Issue	Diagnostic Command	Example Usage
Interface Status	`ip link show` or `ifconfig`	`ip link show`, `ifconfig`
IP Configuration	`ip addr show` or `ifconfig`	`ip addr show`, `ifconfig`
Testing Connectivity	`ping`	`ping 8.8.8.8`, `ping google.com`
DNS Diagnostics	`nslookup` or `dig`	`nslookup openai.com`, `dig openai.com`

This chart outlines common network connectivity issues and the corresponding diagnostic commands for troubleshooting in Linux.

Hands-On Exercise:

Now, here's an exercise to practice troubleshooting network connectivity issues:

Simulate a connectivity issue:

Disable a network interface using ifconfig or ip command.

Use diagnostic commands (ip link show, ip addr show, ping, nslookup, or dig) to identify and resolve the issue.

Create a DNS-related problem:

Modify DNS settings to an incorrect server in the /etc/resolv.conf file.

Use nslookup or dig command to diagnose the DNS resolution problem and rectify the settings.

By completing this exercise, you'll gain practical experience in troubleshooting network connectivity issues and be better equipped to resolve common problems in your Linux environment.

Troubleshooting network connectivity issues requires patience and methodical examination. By practicing these diagnostic commands, you'll develop the skills needed to identify and resolve network problems effectively, ensuring seamless communication across your Linux system!

CHAPTER 8:
SHELL SCRIPTING AND AUTOMATION

Shell scripting involves writing sets of commands in a scripting language (like Bash) that the shell (command-line interface) can interpret and execute. It's like creating a series of instructions or a script to automate tasks on a computer running a Unix-based operating system, such as Linux.

Shell Scripting:

Definition: It's the process of writing a sequence of commands for the shell to execute.

Purpose: To automate repetitive tasks, perform system configurations, manage files, and more.

Language: Often done using scripting languages like Bash, which is the default shell for many Unix-based systems.

Automation:

Definition: The process of automating tasks to reduce human intervention and make processes more efficient.

Role: Automation allows repetitive tasks or complex processes to be executed automatically without continuous manual intervention.

Benefits: Increases productivity, reduces errors, and streamlines workflows by automating routine tasks.

Shell scripting and automation are powerful tools in the Linux environment, offering the ability to create customized scripts that automate tasks, manage configurations, and perform various system operations, thereby making day-to-day operations more efficient and less error-prone.

Understanding shell scripting and automation is like having the ability to create your own personalized assistant that performs tasks according to your instructions, freeing you from repetitive manual work and enhancing productivity in your Linux environment.

Introduction to shell scripting: bash scripting basics

Imagine shell scripting as composing a series of instructions for your Linux system to perform automatically. In this chapter, I'll guide you through the fundamentals of Bash scripting, empowering you to automate tasks and streamline your workflow efficiently.

Understanding Bash Scripts:

What is Bash? Bash (Bourne Again SHell) is a widely-used shell in Linux, offering a command-line interface for users to interact with the system.

Scripting Basics: Bash scripting involves writing a sequence of commands that the shell can execute in a sequential manner.

Writing Bash Scripts:

Creating a Script: I use a text editor like nano or vim to write Bash scripts with a .sh file extension (e.g., myscript.sh).

Shebang Line: Start the script with a shebang (#!/bin/bash) to specify the interpreter.

Executing Bash Scripts:

Running Scripts: After creating a Bash script, I make it executable using the chmod command (chmod +x myscript.sh).

Executing Scripts: Run the script by entering its name in the terminal (./myscript.sh).

Visual Representation in Chart:

Let's create a chart to visualize the key components of Bash scripting:

Concept	Description	Example
Bash Scripting	Writing a sequence of commands	`#!/bin/bash`
Creating Scripts	Using a text editor to write scripts	`nano myscript.sh`
Executing Scripts	Making scripts executable and running	`chmod +x myscript.sh`, `./myscript.sh`

This chart outlines the core concepts and actions involved in Bash scripting, providing a visual guide to understanding the basics.

Hands-On Exercise:

Now, let's practice creating and running a simple Bash script:

Create a Bash script:

Open a text editor (nano or vim) and create a new file named myfirstscript.sh.

Add a few commands (e.g., echo, ls, pwd) to the script file.

Make the script executable and run it:

Use chmod +x myfirstscript.sh to make the script executable.

Execute the script by entering ./myfirstscript.sh in the terminal.

This exercise will provide hands-on experience in creating and running a basic Bash script, solidifying your understanding of Bash scripting fundamentals.

Shell scripting is like crafting a set of custom instructions for your Linux system, enabling automation and simplification of tasks. By practicing these basics, you'll gain the skills needed to create powerful Bash scripts and streamline your workflow efficiently!

Writing simple scripts for automation and task scheduling

Let's delve into the realm of writing simple scripts for automation and task scheduling in Linux. I'll guide you through the basics, visualize key concepts, and then provide a hands-on exercise to reinforce your learning.

Writing Simple Scripts for Automation and Task Scheduling

Hey there! Imagine creating your own digital assistant in Linux that can perform tasks automatically according to your instructions. That's the power of writing simple scripts for automation and scheduling tasks. In this chapter, I'll walk you through the basics of scripting, empowering you to automate routine tasks and schedule operations effortlessly.

Understanding Scripting Basics:

Scripting Language: I use scripting languages like Bash to write simple scripts, comprising a sequence of commands.

Purpose: Scripting allows automation of repetitive tasks, simplifying complex operations and enhancing productivity.

Writing Simple Scripts:

Script Creation: I create scripts using a text editor (such as nano or vim) and save them with a .sh extension (e.g., myscript.sh).

Shebang Line: The script starts with a shebang (#!/bin/bash) to specify the interpreter.

Automation and Task Scheduling:

Automating Tasks: Scripts enable automation by executing a series of predefined commands without manual intervention.

Task Scheduling: Tools like cron allow scheduling script execution at specific times or intervals.

Visual Representation in Chart:

Let's create a chart to visualize the key components of scripting for automation and task scheduling:

Concept	Description	Example
Scripting Language	Writing scripts for automation	`#!/bin/bash`
Script Creation	Using text editors to create scripts	`nano myscript.sh`
Automation	Automating tasks with scripts	`./myscript.sh`
Task Scheduling	Scheduling script execution	`cron: 0 3 * * * /path/to/myscript.sh`

This chart outlines the core concepts and actions involved in writing simple scripts for automation and scheduling tasks in Linux.

Hands-On Exercise:

Now, let's dive into a hands-on exercise to practice writing and scheduling a simple script:

Create a Bash script:

Open a text editor and create a new file named daily_backup.sh.

Write commands to perform a backup operation (e.g., copying files to a backup directory).

Schedule script execution with cron:

Use crontab -e to edit the cron table.

Add an entry to schedule the daily_backup.sh script to run daily at a specific time.

By completing this exercise, you'll gain practical experience in writing a simple script for automation and scheduling its execution using cron.

Writing simple scripts for automation and scheduling tasks is like having your personal assistant handling routine chores in your Linux environment. By practicing these basics, you'll harness the power of scripting to automate tasks and streamline operations effortlessly!

Using loops, conditionals, and functions in shell scripting

Imagine having the ability to create dynamic and flexible scripts that can handle varying conditions and perform repetitive tasks efficiently. That's the power of incorporating loops, conditionals, and functions in shell scripting. In this chapter, I'll walk you through these fundamental concepts, empowering you to write more versatile and powerful scripts.

Understanding Loops:

For Loops: These loops execute a set of commands a specified number of times, iterating through a range or a list of items.

While Loops: These loops execute commands as long as a specified condition is met.

Implementing Conditionals:

if Statements: Conditionals allow executing commands based on specified conditions (if, elif, else).

Comparison Operators: Using operators like -eq, -ne, -lt, -gt, -le, -ge for comparisons.

Embracing Functions:

Creating Functions: Functions allow grouping commands for reuse and modularity in scripts.

Calling Functions: Invoke functions by their name to execute a series of commands.

Visual Representation in Chart:

Let's create a chart to visualize the usage of loops, conditionals, and functions in shell scripting:

Concept	Description	Example
For Loops	Execute commands a specified number of times	`for i in {1..5}; do echo "Iteration $i"; done`
While Loops	Execute commands while a condition is true	`while [ $i -le 5 ]; do echo "Iteration $i"; done`
if Statements	Execute commands based on conditions	`if [ $i -eq 5 ]; then echo "Reached 5"; fi`
Comparison Operators	Operators for conditional comparisons	`$a -eq $b`, `$x -lt $y`, `$var1 != $var2`
Functions	Grouping commands for reuse	`my_function() { commands... }`
Calling Functions	Invoke functions by name	`my_function`

This chart outlines the key concepts and commands related to loops, conditionals, and functions in shell scripting, providing a visual reference for easy understanding.

Hands-On Exercise:

Now, let's put these concepts into practice with a hands-on exercise:

Using Loops:

Create a Bash script that uses a for loop to display numbers from 1 to 5.

Implementing Conditionals:

Write a script that utilizes an if statement to check if a user input number is greater than or equal to 10.

Embracing Functions:

Define a function that takes two parameters and prints their sum.

Invoke the function with different arguments to demonstrate its functionality.

By completing this exercise, you'll gain practical experience in incorporating loops, conditionals, and functions into your shell scripts, enhancing their flexibility and usefulness.

Using loops, conditionals, and functions in shell scripting is like having a toolkit of versatile tools to craft dynamic and responsive scripts. By practicing these concepts, you'll enhance the capabilities of your scripts, making them adaptable to various scenarios in your Linux environment!

CHAPTER 9:
SYSTEM ADMINISTRATION TASKS

As a Linux system administrator, your responsibilities typically involve a wide range of tasks related to maintaining, securing, and optimizing Linux-based systems.

Introduction to system administration roles and responsibilities

Let's delve into the crucial domain of system administration roles and responsibilities. I'll explain the key aspects, visualize their importance, and provide a hands-on exercise to reinforce your understanding.

Introduction to System Administration Roles and Responsibilities

Hey there! As a system administrator, I play a vital role in ensuring the smooth operation of computer systems within an organization. Let's explore the roles and responsibilities that define this critical position and the essential skills required to excel in this domain.

Understanding System Administration:

Role Definition: System administrators are responsible for managing, maintaining, and securing computer systems and networks.

Scope of Work: Their tasks range from hardware and software setup to network configuration and security maintenance.

Key Responsibilities:

System Configuration: Installing and configuring operating systems, applications, and hardware components.

User Management: Creating and managing user accounts, permissions, and access rights.

Backup and Recovery: Implementing backup solutions and devising recovery strategies to protect data.

Monitoring and Maintenance: Monitoring system performance, conducting routine maintenance, and troubleshooting issues.

Security Management: Implementing security measures, ensuring system integrity, and managing access controls.

Visual Representation in Chart:

Let's create a chart to visualize the key responsibilities and skills of a system administrator:

Responsibility	Description	Essential Skills
System Configuration	Setting up OS, applications, and hardware	OS proficiency, hardware knowledge
User Management	Creating and managing user accounts	User administration, access control
Backup and Recovery	Implementing backup solutions	Data backup strategies, recovery planning
Monitoring and Maintenance	System performance monitoring	Troubleshooting, maintenance routines
Security Management	Implementing se ↓ y measures	Security protocols, access controls

This chart illustrates the key responsibilities of a system administrator along with the essential skills required to fulfill these roles effectively.

Hands-On Exercise:

Now, let's engage in a hands-on exercise to simulate system administration tasks:

System Configuration:

Set up a virtual machine using software like VirtualBox or VMware.

Install a Linux distribution and configure the system with necessary applications.

User Management:

Create multiple user accounts with varying access levels (admin, regular user).

Assign permissions and manage access rights for different user groups.

Backup and Recovery:

Set up a backup solution for critical data on your system (e.g., using rsync or a backup tool).

Simulate a data loss scenario and perform a recovery using your backup solution.

Monitoring and Maintenance:

Use system monitoring tools (e.g., top, htop) to monitor system performance.

Perform routine maintenance tasks (e.g., disk cleanup, updates).

Security Management:

Configure firewall settings to control network traffic.

Implement access controls and user authentication mechanisms.

By completing this exercise, you'll gain practical experience in performing fundamental system administration tasks, enhancing your skills in managing and maintaining computer systems effectively.

System administrators are the backbone of ensuring the reliability, security, and efficiency of computer systems. By embracing these responsibilities and honing the necessary skills, one can excel in this dynamic and crucial role in the realm of technology!

Backup and restore strategies: tar, rsync, cron jobs, etc.

Let's explore the vital realm of backup and restore strategies in Linux, encompassing tools like tar, rsync, cron jobs, and more. I'll explain their significance, visualize their usage, and provide a hands-on exercise to reinforce your understanding.

Backup and Restore Strategies: Tar, Rsync, Cron Jobs, etc.

Hey there! As a system administrator, ensuring data integrity and having robust backup strategies are crucial. Let's delve into various backup and restore tools and techniques in Linux, including tar, rsync, cron jobs, and more, which play pivotal roles in safeguarding critical data.

Understanding Backup Strategies:

Backup Importance: Backups are essential to protect against data loss due to hardware failures, accidental deletions, or system errors.

Backup Types: Full backups copy all data, while incremental backups only save changes since the last backup.

Exploring Backup Tools:

Tar (Tape Archive): It's used for creating archives (tar files) and is versatile for compressing multiple files into a single file.

Rsync (Remote Sync): Rsync efficiently syncs and copies files locally or between systems, reducing data transfer by syncing only changes.

Utilizing Cron Jobs:

Cron Scheduler: cron is a task scheduler in Linux that automates recurring tasks (like backups) at specified intervals.

Cron Jobs for Backups: Configuring cron jobs to schedule automatic backups at regular intervals (daily, weekly, etc.).

Visual Representation in Chart:

Let's create a chart to visualize backup tools and strategies in Linux:

Tool	Description	Usage
Tar	Creating and managing archives	`tar -cvf backup.tar /path/to/directory`
Rsync	Efficient file synchronization	`rsync -av /source /destination`
Cron Jobs	Automating backup tasks with scheduler	`0 2 * * * /path/to/backup_script.sh`
Backup Types	Full vs. Incremental backups	`tar -cvf backup_full.tar /data`, `rsync ...`

This chart visualizes the key backup tools, their descriptions, and usage examples, providing a quick reference guide for backup strategies in Linux.

Hands-On Exercise:

Now, let's engage in a hands-on exercise to practice backup and restore strategies:

Tar Archiving:

Create a tar archive of a specific directory containing files (tar -cvf backup.tar /path/to/directory).

Extract the contents of the archive to a different location (tar -xvf backup.tar -C /extract/path).

Rsync Synchronization:

Sync two directories using rsync and ensure that changes in the source directory reflect in the destination directory (rsync -av /source /destination).

Cron Jobs for Automated Backups:

Create a shell script that performs a backup operation.

Configure a cron job to execute this script at a specified interval (e.g., daily).

By completing this exercise, you'll gain practical experience in utilizing tar, rsync, and cron jobs for backup and restore strategies in Linux, enhancing your skills in data protection and management.

Backup and restore strategies are critical for maintaining data integrity and minimizing the risk of data loss. By leveraging these tools and techniques, one can ensure robust data protection in a Linux environment!

Managing system services:
systemctl, service, init.d scripts

Let's delve into the critical domain of managing system services in Linux, covering tools like systemctl, service, and init.d scripts. I'll explain their significance, visualize their usage, and provide a hands-on exercise to reinforce your understanding.

Managing System Services: systemctl, service, init.d Scripts

As a system administrator, ensuring proper management of system services is crucial for maintaining system stability and functionality. Let's explore the tools and techniques used in Linux, including systemctl, service, and init.d scripts, which play pivotal roles in managing services effectively.

Understanding System Services:

Definition: System services are background processes that run continuously, providing essential functionality to the operating system.

Types of Services: Services include network services, daemons, servers, and more, each serving specific purposes.

Exploring Service Management Tools:

Systemctl: systemctl is a command-line utility for controlling system services in modern Linux distributions using systemd.

Service Command: The service command is used to manage services, mainly for systems that use the traditional SysV init system.

Init.d Scripts: The /etc/init.d/ directory contains scripts used to start, stop, and manage services in older Unix-like systems.

Systemctl Usage:

Starting and Stopping Services: Use systemctl start <service> and systemctl stop <service> to respectively start and stop services.

Enabling Services: Enable services to start automatically at boot using systemctl enable <service>.

Service Command:

Start, Stop, and Restart: Use service <service> start/stop/restart commands to manage services.

Status Checking: Check the status of a service with service <service> status.

Init.d Scripts Usage:

Start and Stop Services: Execute /etc/init.d/<service> start/stop to respectively start and stop services.

Restarting Services: Use /etc/init.d/<service> restart to restart a service.

Visual Representation in Chart:

Let's create a chart to visualize the usage of systemctl, service, and init.d scripts in managing system services:

Tool/Command	Description	Usage
systemctl	Systemd service management utility	`systemctl start/stop/enable <service>`
service	Manage services using traditional SysV init	`service <service> start/stop/restart/status`
init.d Scripts	Legacy scripts for service management	`/etc/init.d/<service> start/stop/restart`

This chart illustrates the key service management tools, their descriptions, and usage examples, providing a quick reference guide for managing system services in Linux.

Hands-On Exercise:

Now, let's engage in a hands-on exercise to practice managing system services:

Using systemctl:

Start and stop a service using systemctl start <service> and systemctl stop <service>.

Enable a service to start automatically on boot with systemctl enable <service>.

Service Command:

Use the service command to start, stop, and check the status of a service (service <service> start/stop/status).

Init.d Scripts:

Access the /etc/init.d/ directory and execute scripts to start, stop, and restart services (/etc/init.d/<service> start/stop/restart).

By completing this exercise, you'll gain practical experience in using systemctl, service, and init.d scripts for managing system services in Linux, enhancing your skills in service administration.

Managing system services is a crucial aspect of maintaining a Linux system's functionality. By leveraging these tools and techniques, one can efficiently control and maintain services, ensuring system reliability and performance!

Let's expand further on managing system services in Linux, diving deeper into systemctl, service, and init.d scripts, exploring their functionalities and providing additional insights.

Understanding systemctl, service, and init.d Scripts in System Service Management

As a system administrator, mastering the tools for managing system services is crucial for maintaining system stability and performance. Let's delve deeper into systemctl, service, and init.d scripts, understanding their nuances and their roles in service management.

systemctl: Systemd Service Management

Service Control: systemctl provides comprehensive control over services, including starting, stopping, enabling at boot, and checking the status of services.

Unit Files: Systemd uses unit files (ending with .service) to define and control services, ensuring better system initialization and management.

Advanced systemctl Operations:

Reloading Services: Use systemctl reload <service> to instruct a service to reload its configuration without stopping.

Restart vs. Reload: restart stops and starts a service, while reload only reloads its configuration.

service Command:

SysV Init System: The service command is essential for systems using the traditional SysV init system.

Compatibility: service provides compatibility with legacy scripts and manages service operations similarly to systemctl.

init.d Scripts:

Legacy Support: /etc/init.d/ houses legacy scripts that start, stop, and manage services in older Unix-like systems.

Compatibility with SysV: These scripts support commands like start, stop, restart, and status for service management.

System Service Management Chart:

Let's expand our previous chart to include more details:

Tool/Command	Description	Usage
systemctl	Systemd service management utility	`systemctl start/stop/enable <service>`
		`systemctl reload <service>`
service	Manage services using traditional SysV init	`service <service> start/stop/restart/status`
init.d Scripts	Legacy scripts for service management	`/etc/init.d/<service> start/stop/restart`

Hands-On Exercise (Advanced):

Let's take our hands-on exercise a step further:

Systemctl Reload Operation:

Pick a service and perform a reload operation (systemctl reload <service>).

Observe how the service reconfigures without stopping, ensuring uninterrupted service availability.

Service Command with Compatibility:

Use service to manage a service that's also controllable via systemctl.

Compare and contrast the functionalities and outputs between the two commands.

Init.d Script Handling:

Access /etc/init.d/ and inspect an init.d script.

Execute the script to start, stop, or restart a service and observe the behavior.

By delving deeper into systemctl, service, and init.d scripts and practicing these advanced operations, you'll gain a comprehensive understanding of managing system services in Linux, empowering you with more refined service administration skills.

Mastering systemctl, service, and init.d scripts is pivotal for system administrators to efficiently control and maintain services, ensuring seamless operation and optimal performance in a Linux environment!

CHAPTER 10:
SECURITY AND PERMISSIONS

in Linux, security and permissions are fundamental aspects governing access control to files, directories, and system resources.

Understanding and managing Linux permissions are critical to ensuring system security and preventing unauthorized access to sensitive data or system resources. Regular audits and best practices contribute to a more secure Linux environment.

Understanding Linux file permissions and ownership

Understanding file permissions and ownership in Linux is fundamental for maintaining security and access control. Let's explore this topic in-depth, covering the concepts of permissions, ownership, and their significance. I'll provide visual aids and a hands-on exercise to solidify your understanding.

Understanding Linux File Permissions and Ownership

Hey there! As a system administrator, ensuring proper management of file permissions and ownership is crucial for maintaining system security and controlling access to files and directories in a Linux environment. Let's dive deep into these concepts.

File Permissions Overview:

Definition: File permissions determine who can read, write, or execute a file or directory.

Permission Types: Permissions are categorized for three entities: user (owner), group, and others.

Permission Types and Notations:

Read (r): Allows reading and viewing the contents of a file or directory.

Write (w): Enables modification, editing, or deletion of a file or directory.

Execute (x): Permits execution of a file or traversal of a directory.

Understanding Permission Representation:

Symbolic Notation: Displayed as a series of letters (rwx), representing permission types for owner, group, and others.

Numeric Notation: Represented as octal numbers (0-7), where each digit corresponds to permission types for owner, group, and others.

File Ownership:

Owner: The user who created the file, having the most control over it, including changing permissions.

Group: A set of users sharing common permissions, allowing the owner to grant specific access to this group.

Others: All users who aren't the owner or part of the group.

Visualizing File Permissions Chart:

Let's create a chart to visualize file permissions and their representation in Linux:

Permission Type	Symbolic Notation	Numeric Notation
Read	`r`	4
Write	`w`	2
Execute	`x`	1

Hands-On Exercise:

Now, let's delve into a hands-on exercise to practice setting file permissions:

Using Symbolic Notation:

Permissions

```
chmod octal file - change permissions of file
4 - read (r)
2 - write (w)
1 - execute (x)
order: owner/group/world
chmod 777 :- rwx for everyone
chmod 755 :- rw for owner, rx for group world
```

Create a file and set its permissions using symbolic notation (e.g., chmod u+rwx,g+rw,o-rwx file.txt).

Observe how these permissions impact access for the owner, group, and others.

Applying Numeric Notation:

Create another file and set its permissions using numeric notation (e.g., chmod 754 file2.txt).

Compare the permissions set using symbolic and numeric notations.

File Ownership Management:

Change the ownership of a file using chown command, transferring it to a different user or group.

Observe the changes in ownership and its impact on file access.

By practicing these exercises, you'll gain a deeper understanding of Linux file permissions and ownership, allowing you to control access to files and directories effectively.

Understanding file permissions and ownership is crucial for maintaining a secure and organized Linux system. By grasping these concepts and practicing with various permission settings, you'll enhance your skills in managing access control within a Linux environment!

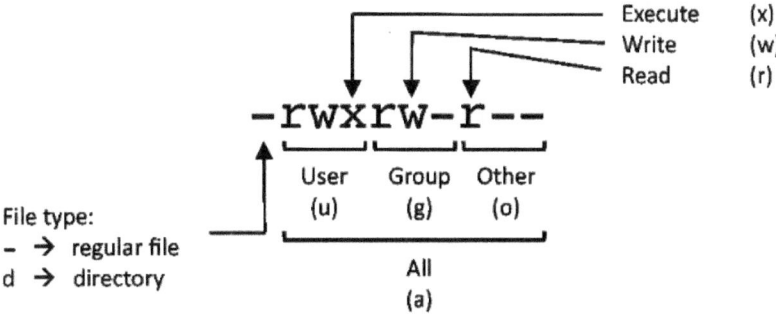

User authentication and managing sudo access

I'll provide a comprehensive explanation on user authentication and managing sudo access in Linux, including visual aids and a hands-on exercise to reinforce your understanding.

User Authentication and Managing Sudo Access in Linux

Hey there! As a system administrator, ensuring secure user authentication and managing sudo access are pivotal for maintaining system integrity and controlling administrative privileges in a Linux environment. Let's explore these topics in depth.

Understanding User Authentication:

User Accounts: Each user in Linux has a unique account associated with a username and password.

Password Authentication: Users are authenticated by providing a correct password linked to their account.

Password Policies:

Password Strength: Encouraging strong passwords with a mix of characters, numbers, and symbols.

Password Aging: Implementing policies to enforce password expiration and periodic changes.

Managing Sudo Access:

Sudo Command: sudo (SuperUser Do) allows users to execute commands with elevated privileges.

Sudoers File: Configuration file (/etc/sudoers) defining who can use sudo and which commands they can execute.

Sudo Access Levels:

Root Access: Grants full administrative privileges, allowing users to execute any command as the superuser.

Specific Command Access: Limits users to running only specified commands with elevated privileges.

Visualizing Sudo Access Levels Chart:

Let's create a chart to visualize sudo access levels in Linux:

Sudo Access Level	Description	Example Usage
Root Access	Full administrative privileges	`sudo su -` (switch to root)
Specific Commands	Limited access to predefined commands	`sudo systemctl restart apache2`

Hands-On Exercise:

Let's engage in a hands-on exercise to practice user authentication and sudo access management:

User Account Management:

Create a new user account using adduser command and set a strong password.

Modify password aging policies using chage to enforce password expiration.

Sudo Configuration:

Add the newly created user to the sudo group or grant sudo access by modifying the /etc/sudoers file using visudo.

Restrict specific commands for the user by editing sudoers file entries.

Testing Sudo Access:

Login with the newly created user and execute commands with elevated privileges using sudo.

Verify if the user can perform root-level tasks or limited to specific commands.

By performing these exercises, you'll gain practical experience in user authentication, password management, and controlling sudo access in Linux, enhancing your skills in maintaining system security and managing administrative privileges effectively.

User authentication and managing sudo access are critical aspects of Linux system administration. By mastering these concepts and practices, you'll be adept at ensuring secure user access and controlling administrative capabilities within a Linux environment!

Basic security practices: Firewalls, SELinux/AppArmor, SSH security

I'll provide a comprehensive explanation on basic security practices in Linux, covering firewalls, SELinux/AppArmor, SSH security, and include a chart and a hands-on exercise to reinforce your understanding.

Basic Security Practices in Linux: Firewalls, SELinux/AppArmor, SSH Security

Hey there! As a system administrator, implementing robust security measures is crucial for safeguarding Linux systems from potential threats. Let's explore fundamental security practices encompassing firewalls, SELinux/AppArmor, and SSH security.

Understanding Firewalls:

Firewall Functionality: Firewalls act as barriers, filtering network traffic to protect systems from unauthorized access or malicious traffic.

Firewall Types: Linux utilizes tools like iptables or firewalld for managing firewall rules.

SELinux/AppArmor for Mandatory Access Control:

Security-Enhanced Linux (SELinux): Provides a set of security rules to enforce mandatory access control policies.

AppArmor: An alternative to SELinux, offering security profiles for individual applications to restrict their actions.

SSH Security:

Secure Shell (SSH): A protocol for secure remote access and communication between systems.

SSH Security Measures: Use key-based authentication, disable root login, and implement IP whitelisting to enhance SSH security.

Visualizing Security Practices Chart:

Let's create a chart to visualize basic security practices in Linux:

Security Practice	Description	Example Usage
Firewalls	Filtering network traffic	`iptables`, `firewalld`
SELinux/AppArmor	Mandatory access control	`semanage`, `apparmor`
SSH Security	Secure remote access	Key-based authentication, IP whitelisting

Hands-On Exercise:

Let's engage in a hands-on exercise to practice basic security practices:

Firewall Configuration:

Use iptables or firewalld to set up basic firewall rules.

Configure rules to allow/deny specific traffic (e.g., block incoming SSH access except from specific IP).

SELinux/AppArmor Implementation:

Enable and configure SELinux or AppArmor on your system.

Create security policies to restrict access for specific applications or services.

SSH Security Measures:

Configure SSH to use key-based authentication instead of passwords.

Implement IP whitelisting to restrict SSH access to specific IP addresses.

By completing these exercises, you'll gain practical experience in implementing basic security practices in Linux, enhancing your skills in protecting systems from potential threats and unauthorized access.

Implementing basic security practices is paramount for ensuring the safety and integrity of Linux systems. By mastering firewalls, SELinux/AppArmor, and SSH security measures, you'll fortify your system against various security risks!

CHAPTER 11:
ADVANCED TOPICS AND FURTHER LEARNING

Linux, an open-source operating system, offers various advanced topics and avenues for further learning.

Introduction to virtualization and containerization: Docker, VirtualBox, etc.

let's dive into the topic of virtualization and containerization in Linux, covering tools like Docker, VirtualBox, and more. I'll provide an extensive explanation, a chart for visualization, and a hands-on exercise to bolster your understanding.

Introduction to Virtualization and Containerization: Docker, VirtualBox, and More

Hey there! As a system administrator, understanding virtualization and containerization is vital for optimizing resource utilization, enhancing scalability, and simplifying application deployment. Let's explore these concepts, including Docker, VirtualBox, and other virtualization/containerization tools.

Understanding Virtualization:

Virtualization Basics: The process of creating virtual instances (Virtual Machines - VMs) that emulate physical hardware.

Types of Virtualization: Includes full virtualization (VirtualBox, VMware) and para-virtualization (Xen) methods.

Introducing Docker and Containerization:

Containerization: A lightweight form of virtualization, allowing applications to run in isolated environments called containers.

Docker: A popular containerization platform for creating, deploying, and managing containers.

Virtualization vs. Containerization:

Resource Utilization: Virtualization creates complete VMs, each with its OS, while containers share the host OS, resulting in lower resource overhead.

Isolation: VMs provide stronger isolation between instances, whereas containers share the host kernel but offer lightweight isolation.

Virtualization and Containerization Tools:

VirtualBox: A powerful open-source virtualization tool for running VMs on a host system.

Docker: A containerization platform using container images to create and deploy applications efficiently.

Visualizing Virtualization and Containerization Chart:

Let's create a chart to visualize the differences between virtualization and containerization:

Aspect	Virtualization	Containerization
Resource Utilization	Higher resource overhead (full VMs)	Lower resource overhead (shared host kernel)
Isolation	Stronger isolation between VMs	Lightweight isolation (shared host OS)
Examples	VirtualBox, VMware, Xen	Docker, Podman, Kubernetes

Hands-On Exercise:

Let's delve into a hands-on exercise to practice virtualization and containerization:

Using VirtualBox for VMs:

Install VirtualBox and create a virtual machine (VM) with a Linux OS.

Configure VM settings, allocate resources, and explore VM management options.

Docker Containerization:

Install Docker and run a containerized application (e.g., a web server) using Docker images from the Docker Hub.

Manage containers, create custom images, and explore Docker networking.

Comparative Analysis:

Compare resource consumption between a VM (VirtualBox) and a container (Docker).

Analyze resource utilization differences and isolation levels.

By completing these exercises, you'll gain practical experience in virtualization with VirtualBox and containerization with Docker, enhancing your skills in utilizing these technologies for efficient resource management and application deployment.

Understanding virtualization and containerization is pivotal for modern system administrators. By mastering tools like VirtualBox and Docker, you'll be adept at leveraging these technologies to streamline operations and improve application deployment processes!

Exploring cloud computing with Linux: AWS, Azure, GCP

Let's explore cloud computing with a focus on major cloud service providers like AWS (Amazon Web Services), Azure (Microsoft Azure), and GCP (Google Cloud Platform). I'll provide an extensive explanation, a chart for visualization, and a hands-on exercise to deepen your understanding.

Exploring Cloud Computing with Linux: AWS, Azure, GCP

Hey there! As a system administrator, delving into cloud computing with major service providers like AWS, Azure, and GCP offers unparalleled scalability, flexibility, and resource management. Let's dive into the world of cloud computing and explore these platforms.

Understanding Cloud Computing:

Cloud Computing Basics: It involves delivering computing services (servers, storage, databases, networking, etc.) over the internet.

Key Attributes: On-demand access, scalability, pay-as-you-go pricing, and resource pooling.

Introducing AWS, Azure, and GCP:

Amazon Web Services (AWS): A comprehensive cloud services platform offering a vast array of tools and services for various business needs.

Microsoft Azure: Microsoft's cloud platform providing a wide range of services like computing, storage, databases, and more.

Google Cloud Platform (GCP): Google's cloud services platform offering infrastructure, data analytics, and machine learning capabilities.

Comparison of AWS, Azure, and GCP:

Service Offerings: Each platform provides a suite of services like compute, storage, databases, networking, AI/ML, etc.

Pricing Models: Different pricing structures and billing methods across platforms.

Ecosystem Integration: Integration with other tools and services within their respective ecosystems.

Visualizing Cloud Computing Providers Chart:

Let's create a chart to visualize the comparison between AWS, Azure, and GCP:

Aspect	AWS	Azure	GCP
Service Offerings	Broad range of services and tools	Diverse services portfolio	Emphasis on data analytics, AI/ML
Pricing	Various pricing models and options	Flexible pricing structures	Customizable pricing plans
Ecosystem	Integrated with Amazon ecosystem	Integration with Microsoft tools	Part of the Google Cloud ecosystem

Hands-On Exercise:

Let's engage in a hands-on exercise to explore these cloud platforms:

AWS Exploration:

Sign up for an AWS account and navigate through the AWS Management Console.

Deploy a simple EC2 (Elastic Compute Cloud) instance and explore storage options like S3 (Simple Storage Service).

Azure Experience:

Create an Azure account and navigate the Azure portal.

Provision a virtual machine and explore Azure storage services like Blob storage.

GCP Exploration:

Set up a GCP account and navigate the GCP Console.

Deploy a Compute Engine instance and explore GCP's BigQuery for data analytics.

By completing these exercises, you'll gain practical experience in exploring AWS, Azure, and GCP, enabling you to understand their interfaces, services, and functionalities for efficient utilization in your projects.

Exploring cloud computing with major service providers like AWS, Azure, and GCP opens up vast opportunities for system administrators. By familiarizing yourself with these platforms, you'll be equipped to leverage the benefits of cloud computing for diverse business needs!

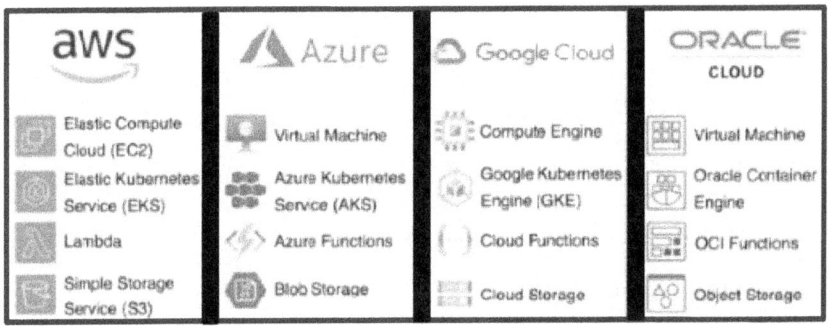

Recommended resources and next steps for advancing Linux skills

let's dive into recommended resources and next steps for advancing Linux skills. I'll provide an extensive explanation, a chart for visualization, and a hands-on exercise to help you further your Linux expertise.

Recommended Resources and Next Steps for Advancing Linux Skills

Hey there! As a system administrator, advancing your Linux skills is an ongoing journey that involves continuous learning and exploration. Let's explore recommended resources and strategies to elevate your proficiency in Linux.

Recommended Learning Resources:

Online Courses:

Platforms like Coursera, Udemy, and edX offer comprehensive Linux courses covering various skill levels, from beginner to advanced.

Official Documentation:

Exploring official documentation from Linux distributions (e.g., Ubuntu, CentOS) provides in-depth insights into system administration and specific configurations.

Books and Guides:

Books such as "Linux Pocket Guide" by Daniel J. Barrett or "The Linux Command Line" by William Shotts are excellent resources for mastering Linux commands and concepts.

Community Forums and Blogs:

Engage with the Linux community through forums like Stack Overflow, Reddit's r/linux, and Linux-focused blogs for troubleshooting, insights, and best practices.

Next Steps for Advancing Skills:

Specialization and Certifications:

Pursue specialized certifications like Red Hat Certified Engineer (RHCE) or Linux Foundation Certified System Administrator (LFCS) to validate your skills.

Contributing to Open Source:

Contribute to open-source projects or develop your own projects to apply and enhance your Linux skills practically.

Practice and Lab Environments:

Set up a lab environment using virtualization tools (e.g., VirtualBox) to experiment, test configurations, and simulate real-world scenarios.

Visualizing Recommended Resources Chart:

Let's create a chart to visualize recommended resources for advancing Linux skills:

Resource Type	Description	Examples
Online Courses	Structured courses for various skill levels	Coursera, Udemy, edX
Official Documentation	Comprehensive guides and references	Linux distribution official documentation
Books and Guides	In-depth books and guides	"Linux Pocket Guide", "The Linux Command Line"
Community Forums	Platforms for engaging with the Linux community	Stack Overflow, Reddit's r/linux, blogs

Hands-On Exercise:

Let's engage in a hands-on exercise to apply and reinforce your Linux skills:

Create a Lab Environment:

Set up a virtualized environment using VirtualBox or VMware with multiple Linux distributions (e.g., Ubuntu, CentOS).

Practice tasks like installing packages, configuring network settings, and managing users and permissions across distributions.

Project Development:

Select an open-source project or create a personal project involving Linux system administration or scripting.

Apply learned skills to contribute to the project or build and manage your own project.

By utilizing these recommended resources and following these next steps, you'll advance your Linux skills significantly, allowing you to tackle complex system administration tasks confidently.

Advancing your Linux skills involves continuous learning and hands-on practice. By leveraging recommended resources and pursuing specialized certifications, you'll excel in mastering Linux and become a proficient system administrator!

For further learning:

Online Courses and Tutorials: Platforms like Coursera, Udemy, and Linux Foundation offer courses on various advanced Linux topics.

Books and Documentation: Dive into books like "UNIX and Linux System Administration Handbook" by Nemeth et al., or explore Linux kernel documentation and man pages for in-depth knowledge.

Community Involvement: Engage with the Linux community through forums (like Stack Exchange's Unix & Linux or Reddit's r/linux) or attend local Linux user groups to share knowledge and learn from others.

Hands-on Practice: Setting up personal projects, experimenting with different configurations, contributing to open-source projects, and solving real-world problems on Linux systems are invaluable for skill development.

Remember, Linux is vast and constantly evolving, so staying curious, exploring, and experimenting are crucial for mastering its advanced concepts.

CHAPTER 12:
CASE STUDIES AND PRACTICAL PROJECTS

Real-world case studies illustrating Linux

implementation in various scenarios

Case Studies:

Scenario	Description
Google's Server Infrastructure	Linux powers Google's extensive server infrastructure, supporting billions of search queries daily.
Embedded Systems in Smart Devices	Linux plays a key role in smart devices like smart TVs and home assistants (Alexa, Google Home).
Supercomputing with Linux	Many supercomputers, including IBM's Summit, rely on Linux for scientific research and simulations.
Linux in Automotive Technology	Linux-based systems power onboard computers in vehicles, supporting entertainment and navigation.
Linux in Healthcare Systems	Hospitals use Linux for secure patient record management, ensuring data privacy and accessibility.
Linux's Role in Education	Linux is prevalent in educational settings, used in computer labs and classrooms for teaching tech.

This table summarizes the various scenarios where Linux is employed, showcasing its versatility across industries and technologies.

To add context to the table let's explore, some cool real-world stories of how Linux works its magic in different places:

1. Server Infrastructure at Google:

Ever wondered what powers Google's massive search engine? Linux does! Google's extensive server infrastructure largely runs on a customized version of Linux. It's like the engine that keeps Google's services humming, handling billions of search queries daily.

2. Embedded Systems in Smart Devices:

Think about your smart TV or your home assistant like Alexa or Google Home. Many of these devices rely on Linux to work their smartness. Linux helps these gadgets run smoothly and manage complex tasks efficiently.

3. Supercomputing with Linux:

Ever heard of supercomputers? Linux is the brain behind many of these mega-powerful machines. Take the example of the

IBM-built Summit supercomputer at Oak Ridge National Laboratory, which runs on Linux. It's used for scientific research, climate modeling, and complex simulations.

4. Automotive Tech:

Your car is getting smarter, right? Linux plays a role there too! Automotive giants like Tesla use Linux-based operating systems to power the onboard computers in their vehicles. It helps manage everything from entertainment systems to autonomous driving features.

5. Healthcare Systems and Linux:

In the world of healthcare, Linux is behind the scenes too. Hospitals use Linux-based systems for storing and managing patient records securely. It ensures data privacy and accessibility, crucial for healthcare operations.

6. Linux in Education:

Think of schools and universities. Many educational institutions leverage Linux in their computer labs and classrooms. It's great for students to learn coding, explore technology, and it's cost-effective for educational purposes.

These case studies showcase how Linux is not just an operating system for computers but a powerhouse that drives various technologies we interact with daily.

While these brief glimpses offer insights into Linux's widespread application, there's a vast ocean of stories and applications out there. Each case study unveils how Linux adapts and excels in diverse environments, making it a fundamental force in our tech-driven world!

Practical projects to reinforce learning and apply skills acquired

Let's explore some fun and hands-on projects that can level up your Linux game:

Practical Linux Projects:

1. Set Up a Home Media Server:

Imagine having your personal Netflix! Use Linux to create a home media server. I did this by installing Plex or Emby on a

Linux machine. It's cool to stream movies, music, and photos to any device in your house.

2. Build a Raspberry Pi Project:

Get your hands on a Raspberry Pi! I built a retro gaming console using RetroPie on a Raspberry Pi with Linux. It's super fun playing old-school games on it.

3. Create a Personal Website:

Ever wanted your corner of the internet? I used Linux to set up a web server using Apache or Nginx. Then, I built my website with HTML, CSS, and maybe even learned a bit of server-side scripting with PHP.

4. Home Automation with Linux:

Turn your place into a smart home! Using Linux, I set up home automation with tools like Home Assistant or OpenHAB. It's neat controlling lights, thermostat, and more from my phone.

5. Network Monitoring and Security:

I got into network monitoring and security by setting up a Linux-based tool like Nagios or Zabbix. It's cool monitoring my home network for any issues or intruders.

6. Linux System Administration Challenges:

Test your skills with challenges! Try things like setting up a secure SSH server, configuring firewalls, or optimizing system performance. These hands-on tasks sharpen your sysadmin skills.

7. Dockerize Your Applications:

Learn about containerization! I experimented with Docker on Linux to containerize my applications. It's fascinating how it simplifies deployment and management.

8. Contribute to Open Source Projects:

Join the open-source community! Contributing to Linux-based projects on GitHub or other platforms is an excellent way to learn, collaborate, and give back to the community.

APPENDIX: LINUX COMMAND REFERENCE

Quick reference guide summarizing essential Linux commands and their usage

This book aims to provide a comprehensive understanding of Linux fundamentals suitable for beginners and aspiring Linux enthusiasts. Each chapter progresses logically from basic concepts to more advanced topics, fostering a practical learning approach through hands-on exercises and real-world examples.

Quick Reference Guide for Essential Linux Commands:

Hey there, fellow explorer! Here's a chart to quickly glance at essential Linux commands and their usage. Let's dive in!

Basic Commands:

Command	Function	Usage Example
`ls`	List directory contents	`ls`
`cd`	Change directory	`cd Documents`
`pwd`	Print working directory	`pwd`
`mkdir`	Make directory	`mkdir NewFolder`
`touch`	Create a new file	`touch new_file.txt`
`rm`	Remove/delete file or directory	`rm file.txt`

File Manipulation:

Command	Function	Usage Example
`cat`	Concatenate and display file contents	`cat file.txt`
`cp`	Copy files and directories	`cp file1.txt file2.txt`
`mv`	Move/rename files and directories	`mv file1.txt new_directory/`
`rm`	Remove/delete file or directory	`rm file.txt`

File Permissions:

Command	Function	Usage Example
`chmod`	Change file permissions	`chmod u+x file.sh`
`chown`	Change file owner and group	`chown user:group file.txt`

System Information:

Command	Function	Usage Example
`uname`	Display system information	`uname -a`
`top`	Display system processes	`top`
`df`	Show disk space usage	`df -h`
`free`	Display available memory	`free -h`

Help and Manual:

Command	Function	Usage Example
`man`	Display manual pages	`man ls`
`--help`	Display command-specific help	`ls --help`

This chart summarizes essential Linux commands and their basic usage, making it easy for quick reference and understanding. Remember, practice makes perfect, so feel free to experiment and explore these commands in your Linux journey!

This quick reference guide offers a concise overview of essential Linux commands and their functionalities. Feel free to refer to this chart whenever you need a quick reminder of these commonly used commands!

The way I learn is to practice and then practice some more until I can remember what the commands do and when to use them.

Linux Learning Resources:

Hey, explorer! Learning Linux is an exciting journey, and here's a chart showcasing some fantastic resources to expand your knowledge:

Resource	Description	Website
1. Linux Documentation	Official documentation covering a wide range of topics	Linux Documentation
2. Linux Journey	Interactive tutorials for Linux beginners to advanced users	Linux Journey
3. Linux Academy	Online platform offering courses on various Linux topics	Linux Academy
4. The Linux Command Line	Book by William Shotts - Comprehensive guide to mastering the command line	The Linux Command Line
5. Ubuntu Forums	Community-based support and discussions for Ubuntu users	Ubuntu Forums
6. Red Hat Learning Subscription	Courses and labs by Red Hat for learning Linux and related technologies	Red Hat Learning Subscription

1. https://www.kernel.org/doc/html/latest/
2. https://linuxjourney.com/
3. https://linuxacademy.com/
4. https://linuxcommand.org/tlcl.php
5. https://ubuntuforums.org/
6. https://www.redhat.com/en/services/training/all-courses-exams

Each resource offers unique learning experiences, from official documentation to interactive tutorials and dedicated platforms for courses and community support.

Explore these resources at your own pace and discover the wonders of Linux. Happy learning!

If you still are asking why you should learn or become proficient in Linux well let's see.

The Linux operating system can be found in various items and devices across different domains due to its versatility, reliability, and open-source nature. Some common places where Linux is commonly used include:

Personal Computers: Linux is installed and used as the primary operating system on desktops, laptops, and workstations by individuals and businesses. Popular distributions like Ubuntu, Fedora, and Linux Mint are often used in this domain.

Servers: A significant portion of servers worldwide runs on Linux due to its stability, security features, and flexibility. It powers web servers, database servers, cloud infrastructure (such as those by AWS, Google Cloud, and Azure), and enterprise servers.

Mobile Devices: Linux-based operating systems, such as Android (based on a modified Linux kernel), run on a large number of smartphones and tablets globally. Android is one of the most prevalent mobile operating systems.

Embedded Systems: Linux is used in embedded devices like routers, smart TVs, IoT (Internet of Things) devices, set-top boxes, smartwatches, and home automation systems due to its ability to work efficiently in resource-constrained environments.

Supercomputers: Many of the world's supercomputers and high-performance computing clusters run on Linux distributions. It's preferred for its reliability, performance, and scalability.

Gaming Consoles: Some gaming consoles, like the Sony PlayStation and Valve's Steam Deck, utilize modified versions of Linux or incorporate Linux-based elements.

Automobiles: Linux is increasingly being integrated into automotive systems for in-car entertainment, navigation, and other computing needs within modern vehicles.

Aerospace and Defense: Linux is used in various aerospace and defense applications due to its reliability and customizability, especially in avionics and satellite systems.

Education and Research: Many educational institutions and research facilities use Linux in labs, research clusters, and educational environments due to its academic licensing and support for scientific computing.

The adaptability of Linux and its open-source nature allow it to be customized for a wide range of applications, making it a popular choice across diverse industries and devices.

In conclusion, " MASTERING LINUX " is a call to action. It urges all of us to embrace the mindset of continuous learning, recognizing that the journey of self-improvement is ongoing. As the world evolves, so must our wiliness to embrace the Linux operating system. Through this exploration, my goal was to inspire readers to cultivate a holistic skill set that positions them not just as experts in their fields but as adept navigators of the complex, interconnected tapestry of the ever-changing world of cloud computing.

Kindest regards

Noe Tovar

SCAN FOR AUTHOR PAGE TO ACCESS
OTHER BOOKS BY THIS AUTHOR

Download bonus command line eBook below.